Author's Bio

Brian Fippinger, Managing Director, Q4 Consulting, Inc.

brian@q4-consulting.com

847-458-6799

www.q4-consulting.com

With over 40 years in business, much of it spent in leadership roles at companies such as GE, AT&T, Microsoft, Cap Gemini Ernst & Young, and Deloitte and Touche, and Brian brings a firsthand knowledge of what it takes to lead organizations and individuals through turbulent times. Tying this background to his creativity, honed during his time teaching Improv for Business at Second City and leading an improv troupe, Brian has seen the business from all sides of the table. He brings that experience to his clients and helps them find creative ways for Leaders and their teams to address the ever-changing challenges.

Along the path, Brian has played many roles in many diverse environments. From Actor to Clerk, to Project Manager, to Engineer, to Analyst, to Consultant, to Senior Manager, to Executive, to Business Owner, to Coach. Brian has learned a great deal about leadership and leading with each step of the way. This background, along with his Somatic Coaching certification from the Strozzi Institute, the acknowledged leader in this field, is what he brings to his clients.

Having seen the world of leadership from all these different angles allows Brian to empathize with the challenges and struggles of those leaders, he has the fortune to spend time discussing the issues they face.

- Brian has been a featured speaker at the Conscious Capitalism International Conferences in 2014, 2015 and 2016

- Brian has also spoken on topics such as:
  - Moving from Being Driven by the Urgent to Moving with What is Important.
  - Finding your Passion; Creating your Path; a Leaders Guide to Transitions
  - Using Improv in Business Communications

Brian lives in Oak Park, Illinois, with his wife, Dr. Chris L. Johnson.

Part 1: I do not like the term "The New Normal."
Chapter 1 The New Status Quo

"Whatever happens in the months ahead, we should assume that we will eventually emerge from the current chaos into a differently ordered society, economy, and business environment. A simple return to the way things were before this crisis appears to be extremely unlikely. Too much has been learned. Too much has been endured by too many. And too bright a spotlight has been placed on too many systemic tensions, weaknesses, and failures of the prevailing order."

This quote from the Deloitte whitepaper titled, *"Recharting our course: The evolving focus of business leaders in a challenging world"* written by Eamonn Kelly and Jason Girzadas explains why I hate the term, "the new norm."

There will be nothing "normal" about our work/life for a long time.

Too many things are changing all at once.

Think about the old days, as long ago as a whole four months before I am typing this in July 2020. Just think of your average day, way back then.

You got up, showered, got dressed in your collared shirt, nice pants, shined shoes, and went downstairs to greet your family.

Your two school-aged kids were all ready for the school bus, your partner was on their way out the door to go to a client meeting, and you would grab your coffee and take the kids to where they got their bus on your way to the office.

Can you remember those days of yore?

A tad bit different now, huh?

THIS morning, you got up, maybe you showered, perhaps you didn't.

You threw on a t-shirt, some shorts, and your flip-flops and ambled downstairs.

Your kids were at the kitchen table, headphones on and, (you hoped) attending their on-line class.

The partner was in their office, with the door open, on a Zoom call (NO headphones) with three other people (all from their homes). Meanwhile, on her second screen, they were busily answering emails.

You grabbed your coffee and went downstairs to the basement, where you have put a desk in the family room to act as your remote "office" to start your day.

Sound about right?

Does this sound or feel "normal" to you?

And this is just the start of your day. Let's not go into the masking every time you go to the Starbuck's, the social distancing you practice when you take a walk. The double-dates you have with friends ON ZOOM.

But what can you do, this is the New Status Quo (NSQ). It is just the way it is.

And that is precisely how the Oxford English Dictionary defines the term Status Quo.

Oxford states: Status Quo; The existing state of affairs, especially regarding social or political issues."

So, in other words, the NSQ is what is. It is the time between right now and whenever Normal happens. And it could be years.

In an essay in the World Economic Forum (WEF) entitled "Work: The Pandemic that Stopped the World." Sharan Burrow, General-Secretary, International Trade Union Confederation, Brussels Belgium, states, *"All of these factors require us to push the reset button on our world and to ensure a just transition to a better future. That transition needs to address all the convergent crises....based on the real needs of people for health, economic security, and respect for their human rights.*

How long does will it take to "reset our world?"

The NSQ will be with us for much longer than we want to admit to ourselves and will affect many areas of our lives. Here are just three.

Where we work

Just this morning (27 July 2020), Google announced they would be keeping employees working from home, worldwide, until at least July 2021. **At least, until that time.**

Later in the week, Apple announced that they would not be returning to their offices until the beginning of 2021, at a minimum, while *"Mark Zuckerberg said there's 'no end in sight' for when employees will be able to return to the office."*

This reinforces that the NSQ will be with us for a long time.

Stability of our jobs and our ability to take care of our families

In the same WEF essay I mentioned above, Ms. Burrow predicts, *"And now we have COVID 19 and the very real potential for over 300 million formal economy jobs lost, and 1.5 livelihoods lost in the informal economy. The UN is warning of famine of "biblical proportions."*

Our mental health

Recently, a Google employee posted a poll on the social network Blind asking people if remote work was hurting their mental health?

For those who are unfamiliar with Blind, they describe themselves this way: *"Blind is an **anonymous community app for the workplace**. Our vision in creating this space was to break down professional barriers and hierarchy."*

Blind has an anonymous community of employees from over 70,000 companies, and thousands of startups!

The Google employee got more than 9,700 responses from companies large and small and from all over the globe. Some of their answers:

- Nearly two-thirds of the respondents said they were feeling stressed by working from home.
- More than 80% of the respondents from some of the largest companies on the planet's employees (Facebook, Yahoo, Airbnb LinkedIn, Goldman Sachs, Oracle) stated the same.
- Generally, Blind posts its own polls, so the fact that a Google employee asked this one is unique. Blind described the more than 800 comments as "free-flow emotional responses that show how personal all these obstacles feel."
- A Siemens employee wrote: "I think everyone is starting to feel the pinch. The sad thing is no one knows when this is going to end. That's the most frustrating part."
- A Facebook employee wrote: "I just struggle being alone all day. Feel so down and lonely, the sad thing is no one knows when this is going to end."

THIS is why I hate the term "The New Normal" as a descriptor for the time we are living.

The New Status Quo is a phrase much closer to the truth. New Status Quo = The New What Is.

Part 2: How do we get from the NSQ to the Next Normal (NN)?

Chapter 2: Technology

In their article, **Does Your Company Have a Long-Term Plan for Remote Work?** (HBR 20 July, 2020) Mark W. Johnson and Josh Suskewicz state, *"To know what's "best" for your organization's future when it comes to remote work, you have to put it in the context of all the things that you are looking achieve. In other words, you have to have a conscious aspiration. Then you need to envision the "workforce system" that will make those things possible."*

There are three parts to that workforce system every corporation must address to make the transition from the NSQ to the NN successfully.

- Technology
- Leadership Skills
- Collaboration Process

To address only one or two of these areas won't cut it. The enormity of the disruption that the pandemic caused, the urgency of the moment, requires radical change.

The companies that can find the right blend of these will be the ones that will come into the NN much better than they began the NSQ.

Technology

Technology is the place where most companies have started.

Unfortunately, this is also the place where most companies have ended.

Technology is the foundation that allows us to work remotely as efficiently, or more efficiently, than when we are in the office. However, if all we do is make sure that all our employees have fast internet, access to Zoom (or Team, or Skype, or WhatsApp) and don't change anything else, we have failed both the employees and the company.

You cannot just take how you ran a meeting in the "old days" of 4 months ago and move that to the NSQ. Even if four months ago, you were meeting on-line.

When you look at today's calendar, are you in back-to-back meetings for most of the day? Do you usually begin each session with, "I am sorry for being a few minutes late, because my last call went long."?

Zoom Fatigue

Zoom Fatigue is real, and there are many reasons for it.

In an article published in April 2020 in National Geographic, Julia Sklar gave this example to define the syndrome.

"JODI EICHLER-LEVINE FINISHED teaching a class over Zoom on April 15, and she immediately fell asleep in the guest bedroom doubling as her office. The religion studies professor at Lehigh University in Pennsylvania says that while teaching is always exhausting, she has never "conked out" like that before.

Until recently, Eichler-Levine was leading live classes full of people whose emotions she could easily gauge, even as they navigated difficult topics—such as slavery and the Holocaust—that demand a high level of conversational nuance and empathy. Now, like countless people around the world, the COVID-19 pandemic has thrust her life into a virtual space. In addition to teaching remotely, she's been attending a weekly department happy hour, an arts-and-crafts night with friends, and a Passover seder— all over the videoconferencing app Zoom. The experience is taking a toll.

So many people are reporting similar experiences that it's earned its own slang term, Zoom fatigue, though this exhaustion also applies if you're using Google Hangouts, Skype, FaceTime, or any other video-calling interface. The unprecedented explosion of their use in response to the pandemic has launched an unofficial social experiment, showing at a population scale what's always been true: virtual interactions can be extremely hard on the brain."

Jeff Hancock, the founding director of the Stanford Social Media Lab and a Professor in the Department of Communication at Stanford University, explains one reason for this phenomenon.

"Having a conversation on Zoom is a very different experience than having a conversation in person," he said. "When you're face-to-face, for example, you don't stare directly at someone for long periods of time when they're talking. Now and then, you look away. However, on Zoom, you have an audience - sometimes of multiple people - constantly staring directly back at you. All the while, we are unable to move because we have to keep our head in the frame. It's intense and exhausting, especially if you are doing it many times a day."

But in the NSQ, when "what is" means everything is remote, what can we do about this? We still have to get things done. We still need to meet, even during this crisis.

The Chinese language expresses the word crisis as "危机" (wēi jī), denoting a state of both danger and opportunity. What would it be like if we took this particular crisis as an opportunity to change the way we look at how we work together, starting with the way we meet.

Shorten our meeting times

No meetings should last more than 45 minutes and, if possible, begin at the top or bottom of the hour. The break will allow everyone involved to have fifteen minutes to get up, move around, and not stare at their screens—those things you used to do in between meetings when you were in the office. You have to be diligent about the time. You will defeat the purpose, and lose the opportunity to change, if you only change the allotted calendar time, but not the actual time.

Vary your presentation style

If you have regular meetings with the same individuals (e.g., week sales meetings), try not to use the same style of presenting the information two sessions in a row.

This is where technology comes in to play. Don't be afraid to get creative; after all, we are in the New Status Quo. Nothing is Normal.

Some ideas for your presentations:

Use videos instead of PowerPoint.

By this, I don't mean, take a video of yourself presenting your slide deck.

However, find an internal video that addresses the topic at hand. Look on YouTube for a similar question, and show that.

Perhaps you could record an interview with your boss discussing the topic. (I like this one because you can use a tool (Zoom) to liven up your Zoom meeting.)

The use of video is powerful during the NSQ and will engage the participants in ways that a standard PowerPoint deck cannot.

Use pictures instead of words/charts/graphs.

There are many ways information is encoded in our brain, but these methods generally rely on either visualizations — remembering information as images, or verbalization — remembering information as words. Research has shown that we retain information faster and longer from pictures than we do from words. Our ability to create mental representations is an innate ability we all have.

In the best selling book PEAK, Secrets From the New Science of Expertise, the authors Anders Ericsson and Robert Pool explain it this way.

"Any relatively complicated activity requires holding more information in our heads than short-term memory allows, so we are always building mental representations of one sort or another without even being aware of it. Indeed, without mental representations we couldn't walk (too many muscle movements to coordinate), we couldn't talk (ditto on the muscle movements, plus no understanding of the words), we couldn't live any sort of human life."

There is truth in the adage. Pictures are worth a thousand words. So try going a whole session with just pictures.

Have a roundtable discussion instead of a presentation.

"No decision-making system is going to guarantee corporate success. The strategic decisions that corporations have to make are of mind-numbing complexity. But we know that the more power you give a single individual in the face of complexity and uncertainty, the more likely it is that bad decisions will get made."
— James Surowiecki, *The Wisdom of Crowds*

In the NSQ, how many of the areas of discussion in meetings are straight forward and simple? Not that many, so when you meet, why merely present?

Send out the topics you want to cover a day in advance. List some questions you have on the subjects or points you wish to include, and during the meeting, make it a discussion.

You facilitate the meeting and ensure everyone has a voice in the room.

By doing this, you will ensure the individuals involved are engaged and feeling heard. In turn, you get the wisdom of the crowd, and you are lowering the stress and anxiety of the entire group.

Go old-school: Just have a telephone call.

Give people a break from staring at their monitor and being "on."

Just talk to them. Trust me. I am old enough to remember when talking on the telephone worked just fine.

(NOTE for this suggestion. This option works best for small groups, certainly not with more than four individuals, including the leader.)

Create a podcast.

Studies show that 80% of people will listen to an entire podcast episode, or most of it, indicating that podcast listeners are very engaged in the content. Those same studies show that 37% (104 million) people in the US listened to a podcast in the last month.

The ability to use a technology that people you are working with (more than likely are) already engaged with and is not the usual way the workplace communicates is a powerful way to convey your message.

And the podcast can take many forms.

- Video
- Audio
- Storytelling
- Presentation
- Interviews
- The list goes on

Hidden in the above information on how to present your data, utilizing the different technologies available are the nuances within the technologies.

For example: Have you ever used the "Rooms" feature within Zoom? You can begin by presenting the data on a subject and then break your participants into separate rooms to discuss their ideas for a set amount of time. The feature will bring them back into the main room after time expires, and the group can discuss their findings.

This example is just one of the myriad of options you have available. Utilize the full range of functions available to you.

I can just hear many of you saying, "I know nothing about doing a video/podcast/etc. I just figured out to link my Zoom to my calendar!" I get it. Many of these suggestions are new, will take time to figure out and perfect. There is plenty of guidance out there on YouTube, on vendor websites, other white papers, and from coaches.

Part 2: How do we get from the NSQ to the Next Normal (NN)?

Chapter 3: New Leadership Skills

I started Part 2 off discussing the Technology required during our transition from the NSQ to the NN for two reasons:

1. The technology piece is the most comfortable area to handle. When the rush of Stay at Home order came out, most companies' first response was to ensure that the technical infrastructure was in place to deal with the NSQ of a fully remote workforce.

   Doing this first made complete sense. In-person events now became converted for a virtual audience. People who had seldom worked from home had to establish a home office. All this had to get done as quickly as humanly possible.

2. Technology is foundational to the other two steps, but it is an incomplete solution without the other two.
   a. Leadership Skills
   b. Collaboration Process

Let's start by defining what I mean when I say Leadership Skills.

I define Leadership Skills as the skills required by all employees (and especially Leaders) to survive the stress, anxiety, and confusion we face in the NSQ.

Most companies, and most people in those companies, have always given lip service to most of the skills I believe are vital. Most companies, and most people in those companies, have done a poor job of actually incorporating these soft-skills into their actions.

These two must become embodied within our organizations.

A. Expressing Empathy
B. Deep Listening

Expressing Empathy

Oxford defines empathy as: The ability to understand and *share* the feelings of another.

Before you close the book and walk away, please hear me out about why empathy is one of the skills that we need to have in the NSQ.

First, because people are scared, anxious, and overwhelmed.

An international study by The Sun out the UK found the following:

- 75% of the respondents worried life would never return to normal after COVID 19.
- 59% said they could not use shared workspaces without being scared of contracting or spreading the deadly virus.
- 35% of the respondents said they are afraid of returning to their workplace for fear of infecting their loved ones.
- 63% of the respondents believe their jobs will never revert to pre-pandemic normality.
- Over six in 10 workers believe their boss didn't handle the WFH transition as seamlessly as they could have done.
- 67% of the employed respondents felt that their superiors didn't understand the struggles of remote work when they have kids at home.
- 64% of participants, who are childless, felt they weren't as productive due to heightened stress levels and pandemic anxiety.
- Seven in ten employed people said it would be great to have a work coach as they continue working from the safety of their home.

The elephant in the room is that people are scared and do not think their companies have handled the transition well. That fear is in the background of every interaction they have, and if you ignore that fact, you will have people either burning out, or turning out. Either way, talented people will be sidelined.

So, how do you address those things that people aren't comfortable discussing in a work setting?

It starts with having and showing empathy.

In the January 17, 2020, Recruter.com's The Innovators, described empathy as follows:

"1. Cognitive Empathy

Also known as "perspective-taking," this type of empathy is about understanding another person's emotional state. Employees who show cognitive empathy are able to easily interpret other people's thoughts and feelings, which helps them determine the best way to move forward in difficult situations. Because of this, cognitive empathy is critical for building comfortable, flexible work environments that support all your employees' goals, abilities, and aspirations.

Do not confuse empathy with sympathy. A typical example of empathy is accurately detecting when someone is afraid and needs encouragement. A typical example of sympathy is feeling sorry for someone who has lost a loved one.

Empathy is a skill that you can learn, and you can start by practicing how you behave in your relationships. During conversations, focus your full attention and time on listening and only then doing whatever you can so the person feels understood. To accurately perceive his feelings, you can ask questions: "It sounds like you're feeling dejected. Is that right?" Or, "Is it fair to say that you're feeling optimistic?"

Listening Differently

The next Leadership Skill that is critical to develop is Listening in the NSQ when every conversation is a remote one, is a uniquely different than listening in person. You have to remember you only hear a fraction of what you would in person.

You hear only the words and the tone of the words.

What you are missing is the body language of the speaker. The energy of the speaker. The energy in the room.

You miss all those non-verbal portions of the conversation that are vital to a full understanding of what is said.

So, how do we change the way we listen to compensate for what we can no longer hear?

The first thing we must do will be (in my assessment) the hardest for us to do.

Stop Multi-Tasking

The truth is, you can't multi-task. The brain is just not wired that way. It is just like the laptop I am typing this paper on. It seems like it multi-tasks, in the panel on my screen next to the text I am typing, Grammarly has a little wheel turning, and it tells me it is "Checking," but it isn't really checking as I am typing. It is waiting for me to pause, and then it takes over.

Just like my laptop, if you don't have two brains, you can only do one thing at a time.

In the May 14th, 2014 issue of Psychology Today magazine, Nancy Napier, Ph.D. says it this way in her article, *The Myth of Multitasking*, "*Research in* neuroscience *tells us that the brain doesn't really do tasks simultaneously, as we thought (hoped) it might. In fact, we just switch tasks quickly. Each time we move from hearing music, to writing a text, or talking to someone, there is a stop/start process that goes on in the brain.*

That start/stop/start process is rough on us. Rather than saving time, it costs time (even very small micro seconds). It's less efficient, we make more mistakes, and over time, it can sap our energy."

If you ask yourself, "Do you believe your brain multi-tasks?", most everyone will admit that they cannot. If you could be in the room with those same people while they are on a typical Zoom call, you would see the vast majority of them checking their cellphones, texting, sending emails. In other words, multi-tasking.

"But I heard every word of the call!" they will argue. But were they really listening?

See the clown on the Unicycle? Do you think if you walked across that square talking on your cellphone, you would notice him?

More than 75% of the college-aged people who were walking and talking on their cell phones, didn't.

From the New York Times article on October 22, 2009, *"When asked if they saw the unicycling clown, only 8% spontaneously remembered the clown......Then the researchers followed up with a second question: "Did you see the unicycling clown?"....... Only 25 percent of cellphone talkers remembered seeing a clown on a unicycle, according to the report in the journal Applied Cognitive Psychology.*

When you are multi-tasking, you are not performing any of the tasks you are trying to juggle at your top performance, and you are using unwanted energy, which will inevitably add to Zoom Fatigue.

Why am I spending so much time attempting to kill the myth of multi-tasking, you may ask? Because multi-tasking is the number one obstacle to deeply listening to others. And if you aren't deeply listening, it is hard for you to be authentic and empathic. We will cover how to Listen Deeply in a future whitepaper.

Part 2: How do we get from the NSQ to the Next Normal (NN)?

Chapter 4: Collaboration Process

In their July 8 2020 article for the Harvard Business Review (**7 Strategies for Promoting Collaboration in a Crisis**), Heidi K. Gardner and Ivan Matviak conclude, *"Crises like the Covid-19 pandemic highlight the importance of effective collaboration for long-term commercial success. Particularly in a crisis, organizations need to pull together experts with unique, cross-functional perspectives to solve rapidly changing, complex problems that have long-term implications. The diversity of experience allows a group to see risks and opportunities from different angles so that it can generate new solutions and adapt dynamically to changing situations."*

But how do we make this happen? How do we make sure that our teams are working together while they are apart? Can we be assured that everyone understands each other? Are we confident that the entire team understands what success looks like, when they are under the stress of being salesperson, mom, school teacher, caregiver, and leader?

At Q4, we call this process the Core Commitment Process, and it was developed after many years of work by my Partner, Dr. Chris Johnson. I will let her explain the concept in her own words.

"Skillful leaders, effective leaders, exemplary leaders even lead because they cultivate amazing teams.

And they cultivate amazing teams by generating a sense of trust and well-being--the ability for people on the team to bring forth their best efforts.

*We have a process called the **core commitment cycle** that's a powerful, pragmatic & innovative framework where we teach people, call it a frame or process -both, that creates a way for people to create greater commitments & promises to each other.*

We develop a common language around how we're going to work together, so people can bring their best selves into the team.

We do this by crafting promises one to another so that we can have work happen effectively and efficiently.

The core commitment cycle is built on the three elements that create the fabric, three threads that integrate to form the fabric of an amazing team:

1. *Attention*

2. *360 Awareness*

3. *Conversation*

*With mindful attention, we know that **where we put our attention our energy follows***

*With Awareness, we're cultivating full-bodied, fully human awareness, a 360 awareness of **what's in us**, **what's around us**, and lastly **the idea that how we use language, the linguistic functions of how we speak to each other**, are incredibly powerful and underpin our best conversations.*

Attention, awareness, and conversation together create an embodied learning process where we're learning on the job.

***And we know that together, regardless of what technical skills people bring in, what** book knowledge they have from where they came from, their domain of expertise, that in this **core commitment cycle** we're able together to create a new Learning Team that will get work done, to be more accountable to one another, and to ultimately to the organization, to create a culture of care and ethic of care so that everyone's voice is heard and that everyone knows that their ideas are taken into consideration.*

When we're working on the team, this approach results in greater accountability, more efficiency, less rework, a greater sense of psychological safety—the ground for trust, and care.

And we know that people like to work with others that they trust.

*So the **core commitment cycle** is ultimately a process of cultivating and developing trust through how we act, who we are as we show up, and the conversations that we have.*

Taken into consideration when we're working on the team the results greater

accountability more efficiency less rework greater sense of trust in care

and we know that people like to work with others that they trust so this is

ultimately the core commitment cycle is a process of cultivating and

developing trust through how we act who we are as we show up and the

conversations that we have."

So you see, the Core Commitment Cycle (CCC) is what ties the first two areas we talked about, technology and leadership skills together into an efficient and coherent way of working.

Through Mindful Attention, we are present in each moment, focusing on listening profoundly and being on point—no more multi-tasking and missing the clowns.

Using our full selves to be fully aware, we can bring empathy, trust, and understanding to our teams and our peers to collaborate at the highest levels.

By creating a Common Language for the necessary conversation in the NSQ, we will:

- Ensure clarity of the tasks at hand and who is responsible to whom.
- Teams will co-create the conditions of success for the projects and understand why it is essential.
- Be crystal clear in oral, email, text, Slack, and every other form of communication that we are using in the NSQ.
- Heighten the level of accountability, not only to the organization but to each other.
- Learn how to collaborate by making Promises.
- And so much more.

I will not attempt to provide a complete description of the CCC in this book. We will cover the topic in a separate paper. Or, a discussion during our one-hour free consulting.

Combining the CCC, with the technological tools we discussed in Chapter 1 and the Leadership Skills from Chapter 2, an organization will be able to manage the tough road from today's New Status Quo, to the uncertain New Normal.

BIBLIOGRAPHY

Eamonn Kelly and Jason Girzadas
Recharting our course: The evolving focus of business leaders in a challenging world
May 2020
Deloitte
www.deloitte.com

Sharan Burrow
World Economic Forum: Challenges and Opportunities in the Post-COVID-19 World, Chapter 7: Work: The Pandemic that Stopped the World
July 17, 2020
www.weforum.org

Mark W. Johnson and Josh Suskewicz
Does Your Company Have a Long-Term Plan for Remote Work?
Harvard Business Review
July 20, 2020
www.hbr.com

Julia Sklar
Zoom fatigue' is taxing the brain. Here's why that happens.
National Geographic
April 24, 2020
www.nationalgeographic.com

Nancy Napier
The Myth of Multitasking
Psychology Today
May 14, 2014
www.psychologytoday.com

Jeff Hancock
The pressures of remote work are pushing employees into making avoidable mistakes that leave their companies wide open to cyberattack, a new study from a Stanford researcher and cybersecurity company Tessian finds
Business Insider
July 27, 2020
www.businessinsider.com

Anders Ericsson and Robert Pool
PEAK, Secrets From the New Science of Expertise
2016
USA
Houghton, Mifflin, Harcourt Publishing Co.
www.hmhco.com

James Surowieke
The Wisdom of Crowds, Why the Many Are Smarter Than the Few and How Collective Wisdom Shapes Business, Economies, Societies and Nations
2004
Doubleday, Anchor
www.knopfdoubleday.com

Recruter.com's The Innovators
July 17, 2020
www.recruters.com

Tara Parker-Pope
What Clown on a Unicycle? Studying Cellphone Distraction
New York Times
October 22, 2009
www.nyt.com

Heidi K. Gardner and Ivan Matviak
7 Strategies for Promoting Collaboration in a Crisis
Harvard Business Review
July 8, 2020
www.hbr.com

Dr. Chris L. Johnson
The Core Commitment Cycle (video)
YouTube - Q4 Consulting, Inc.
May 3, 2017

Words of Gratitude

I first want to express gratitude to Guillermo Ortega Rance, the CEO of Innovatorio, a leading innovation and collaboration lab in Mexico City, for inviting me to have a Facebook Live conversation with him, that inspired me to write this book.

Secondly, to my friends and colleagues, Kevin Quinn, Ahmed Hedayat, and Nick Blawat, for their wise words and edits to the document.

And, finally, to my Partner, wife and inspiration, Dr. Chris Johnson, for her belief in me and her encouragement.

www.ingramcontent.com/pod-product-compliance
Lightning Source LLC
Chambersburg PA
CBHW030558220526
45463CB00007B/3112